Pebble® Plus

Women in Sports

CANDACE PARKER

by Mary Dunn

CAPSTONE PRESS
a capstone imprint

Pebble Plus is published by Capstone Press
1710 Roe Crest Drive, North Mankato, Minnesota 56003
www.mycapstone.com

Library of Congress Cataloging-in-Publication Data
Cataloging-in-Publication Data is on file with the Library of Congress.
ISBN 978-1-4914-7975-9 (library binding)
ISBN 978-1-4914-8571-2 (paperback)
ISBN 978-1-4914-8577-4 (eBook PDF)

Editorial Credits
Abby Colich, editor; Sarah Bennett, designer; Eric Gohl, media researcher;
Katy LaVigne, production specialist

Photo Credits
Dreamstime: Lukyslukys, cover (background), 1; Getty Images: NBAE/David Sherman,
7; Newscom: Cal Sport Media/Anthony Nesmith, cover, 5, Icon SMI/Christophe Elise, 17,
Icon SMI/Jeffrey Haderthauer, 11, MCT/Chuck Myers, 21, Reuters/John Sommers II, 13,
SportsChrome/Ross Dettman, 9, TASS/Krasilnikov Stanislav, 19; Shutterstock: Chones, 3,
23, Photo Works, 15, studio 55, back cover, 2, 22, 24, Torsak Thammachote, 11 (background),
15 (background), 19 (background), 21 (background)

Note to Parents and Teachers

The Women in Sports set supports national curriculum standards for social
studies related to people, places, and culture. This book describes and illustrates
Candace Parker. The images support early readers in understanding the text.
The repetition of words and phrases helps early readers learn new words. This
book also introduces early readers to subject-specific vocabulary words, which
are defined in the Glossary section. Early readers may need assistance to read
some words and to use the Table of Contents, Glossary, Read More, Internet Sites,
Critical Thinking Using the Common Core, and Index sections of the book.

Printed in the United States of America in North Mankato, Minnesota.
092015 009221CGS16

Table of Contents

A Basketball Family

Candace Parker was born April 19, 1986. She has two older brothers. Candace went to her first basketball game when she was 2 weeks old.

TIMELINE

1986

born in
St. Louis, Missouri

In grade school Candace played soccer. In eighth grade she switched to basketball. Candace's dad was her coach. They practiced anywhere they could dribble a ball.

Candace with her parents, Sara and Larry

School Team Success

Candace played high school basketball in Illinois. She could move quickly. She had great shooting skills. Candace won two state titles with her team.

TIMELINE

1986
born in
St. Louis, Missouri

2003, 2004
wins high school
state titles

Candace's dad taught her how

to slam-dunk a basketball.

She won the 2004 McDonald's

All-American Slam Dunk Contest.

She was the first woman to win.

TIMELINE

1986	2003, 2004	2004
born in St. Louis, Missouri	wins high school state titles	wins McDonald's All-American Slam Dunk Contest

After high school Candace played

for the University of Tennessee.

She broke many school records.

Her team won NCAA titles

in 2007 and 2008.

NCAA stands for National
Collegiate Athletic Association.

TIMELINE

1986	2003, 2004	2004	2007, 2008
born in St. Louis, Missouri	wins high school state titles	wins McDonald's All-American Slam Dunk Contest	wins NCAA titles

Pro Star

The Los Angeles Sparks chose
Candace in the 2008 WNBA Draft.
In 2008 Candace played for the
United States in the Olympics.
The team won a gold medal.

WNBA stands for Women's
National Basketball Association.

TIMELINE

1986	2003, 2004	2004	2007, 2008	2008
born in St. Louis, Missouri	wins high school state titles	wins McDonald's All-American Slam Dunk Contest	wins NCAA titles	begins playing for the Los Angeles Sparks wins first Olympic gold medal

Candace joined a team in Russia in 2010. The team plays after the WNBA season ends. Candace helped the United States win Olympic gold in 2012. She was top scorer and rebounder in the final game.

TIMELINE

1986	2003, 2004	2004	2007, 2008	2008
born in St. Louis, Missouri	wins high school state titles	wins McDonald's All-American Slam Dunk Contest	wins NCAA titles	begins playing for the Los Angeles Sparks
				wins first Olympic gold medal

2010

begins playing on a
team in Russia

2012

wins second
Olympic gold medal

Candace's Russian team won
the league championship in 2013.
Later that year Candace played
in her first WNBA All-Star Game.
She became the season's MVP.

MVP stands for
Most Valuable Player.

TIMELINE

1986	2003, 2004	2004	2007, 2008	2008
born in St. Louis, Missouri	wins high school state titles	wins McDonald's All-American Slam Dunk Contest	wins NCAA titles	begins playing for the Los Angeles Sparks
				wins first Olympic gold medal

2010

begins playing on a
team in Russia

2012

wins second
Olympic gold medal

2013

wins championship with
Russian team

becomes the WNBA's
season MVP

In 2015 Candace was a top

scorer and rebounder for the Sparks.

She is known for being able

to slam-dunk the ball. Candace is

one of the WNBA's top players.

TIMELINE

1986
born in
St. Louis, Missouri

2003, 2004
wins high school
state titles

2004
wins McDonald
All American Slam
Dunk Contest

2007, 2008
wins NCAA titles

2008
begins playing for the
Los Angeles Sparks

wins first Olympic
gold medal

2010

begins playing on a
team in Russia

2012

wins second
Olympic gold medal

2013

wins championship with
Russian team

becomes the WNBA's
season MVP

2015

is a top scorer
and rebounder
for the Los
Angeles Sparks

21

Glossary

All-Star Game—a league game played once a year; the teams are made up of the league's biggest stars

championship—a contest held to find a winner

draft—an event held for teams to choose new people to play for them

dribble—to bounce a basketball off the floor using one hand

league—a group of sports teams that play against each other

MVP—short for Most Valuable Player; an award that goes to the best player in a game or season

pro—short for professional; a person paid for an activity or sport

rebound—to get the ball after a missed shot

record—when something is done better than anyone has ever done it before

season—the time of year in which a sport takes place

slam-dunk—to put the ball through the net with force

title—an award given to the winner of a tournament

Read More

Editors of Sports Illustrated Kids Magazine. *Sports Illustrated Kids Big Book of Who Basketball.* New York: Time Home Entertainment, 2015.

Savage, Jeff. *Super Basketball Infographics.* Super Sports Infographics. Minneapolis: Lerner, 2015.

Schrier, Allyson Valentine. *A Girl's Guide to Basketball.* Get in the Game. North Mankato, Minn.: Capstone Press, 2012.

Internet Sites

FactHound offers a safe, fun way to find Internet sites related to this book. All of the sites on FactHound have been researched by our staff.

Here's all you do:
Visit *www.facthound.com*
Type in this code: 9781491479759

Super-cool stuff! Check out projects, games and lots more at **www.capstonekids.com**

23

Critical Thinking
Using the Common Core

1. Reread the text on page 8. Describe why moving quickly would be an important skill in basketball. (Integration of Knowledge and Ideas)

2. Candace broke school records at the University of Tennessee. Use the Glossary to describe what a record is. (Craft and Structure)

Index